FIFTH WORLD TALES
STORIES FOR ALL CHILDREN
FROM THE MANY PEOPLES
OF AMERICA.

CUENTOS DEL QUINTO MUNDO
CUENTOS DE LOS MUCHOS
PUEBLOS DE AMÉRICA PARA
TODOS LOS NIÑOS.

My Aunt Otilia's Spirits

Los espíritus de mi tía Otilia

WRITTEN BY / ESCRITO POR   RICHARD GARCÍA
ILLUSTRATED BY / ILUSTRADO POR   ROBIN CHERIN & ROGER I REYES
TRANSLATED INTO SPANISH BY / TRADUCIDO AL ESPAÑOL POR   JESÚS GUERRERO REA

CHILDREN'S BOOK PRESS / IMPRENTA DE LIBROS INFANTILES

SAN FRANCISCO , CALIFORNIA

WHEN I WAS A BOY
MY AUNT OTILIA
WOULD VISIT US
EVERY SUMMER.

HER HOME WAS ON
THE ISLAND
OF PUERTO RICO.

SHE WAS TALL, SKINNY,
NEVER SMILED,
AND WORE
A BIG HAT.

CUANDO YO ERA NIÑO,
MI TÍA OTILIA
NOS VISITABA
CADA VERANO.

VENÍA DESDE SU CASA EN
LA ISLA
DE PUERTO RICO.

ERA ALTA, FLACA,
NUNCA SONREÍA
Y LLEVABA
UN GRAN SOMBRERO.

Revised edition © 1987, original edition © 1978 by Children's Book Press/Imprenta de Libros Infantiles.
All rights reserved. Printed in Hong Kong through Interprint, San Francisco.

CIP Data may be found on page 24.

Because there was little room in our house, Aunt Otilia used to share my bed.

And every night, just before I went to sleep, we would hear a knocking on the wall. Three times. And then the bed would begin to shake like there was an earthquake.

4

A CAUSA DE QUE HABÍA POCO ESPACIO
EN NUESTRA CASA, TÍA OTILIA
ACOSTUMBRABA COMPARTIR MI CAMA.

Y CADA NOCHE,
JUSTAMENTE ANTES DE QUE ME DURMIERA,
OÍAMOS UN GOLPETEO
EN LA PARED. TRES VECES.
Y ENTONCES LA CAMA EMPEZABA
A SACUDIRSE COMO SI HUBIERA
UN TERREMOTO.

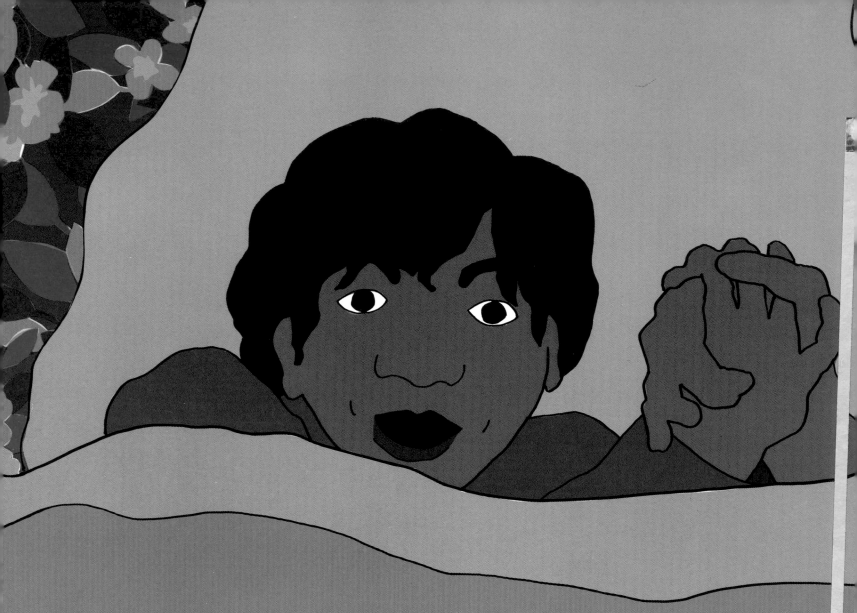

"WHAT'S THAT!" I WOULD CRY OUT, WITH MY EYES GROWING WIDE.
"OH, IT'S NOTHING," MY AUNT OTILIA WOULD SAY.
"IT'S JUST MY SPIRITS. GO TO SLEEP, DEMONIO,"
WHICH WAS HER PET NAME FOR ME AND MEANT "DEVIL."

WHEN SHE WOULD SAY THAT, I WOULD FALL ASLEEP,
STILL HOLDING HER SKINNY HAND.
BUT JUST BEFORE I FELL ASLEEP

—¡QUÉ ES ESO!— GRITABA YO CON LOS OJOS MUY ABIERTOS.
—¡OH, NADA!—, DECÍA MI TÍA OTILIA.
—SON SÓLO MIS ESPÍRITUS. DUÉRMETE, DEMONIO—,
TAL ERA SU NOMBRE CARIÑOSO PARA MÍ.

CUANDO ELLA DECÍA ESO YO ME QUEDABA DORMIDO,
COGIDO FUERTEMENTE DE SU MANO FLACA.
PERO, JUSTAMENTE ANTES DE QUEDARME DORMIDO,

I WOULD HEAR A LOUD CRASH,
LIKE A PILE OF SPOONS FALLING.
AND I WOULD HEAR HER VOICE
IN THE DISTANCE,
"GO TO SLEEP.
ONLY MY SPIRITS.
GO TO SLEEP, DEMONIO."

OÍA UN GRAN ESTRÉPITO,
COMO UN MONTÓN
DE CUCHARAS QUE CAÍAN.
Y OÍA SU VOZ
EN LA DISTANCIA:
_DUÉRMETE...
SON SÓLO MIS ESPÍRITUS.
DUÉRMETE, DEMONIO.

9

WELL, I BEGAN TO WONDER ABOUT MY AUNT OTILIA.
AND ONE NIGHT I PUT CHEWING GUM IN MY EARS,
HOPING THAT IF I DIDN'T HEAR HER VOICE,
I COULD STAY AWAKE AND SEE WHAT ALL THE NOISE WAS.

THAT NIGHT EVERYTHING HAPPENED AS USUAL.
THREE KNOCKS. THE BED SHOOK.
AND I PRETENDED TO SLEEP.

PUES BIEN, EMPECÉ A TENER DUDAS ACERCA DE MI TÍA OTILIA.
Y UNA NOCHE ME PUSE GOMA DE MASCAR EN LOS OÍDOS,
ESPERANDO QUE, AL NO OÍR SU VOZ,
PODRÍA PERMANECER DESPIERTO Y VER A QUÉ SE DEBÍA TODO AQUEL RUIDO.

ESA NOCHE TODO SUCEDIÓ COMO DE COSTUMBRE.
TRES GOLPES. LA CAMA SE SACUDIÓ.
Y YO FINGÍA ESTAR DORMIDO.

11

SUDDENLY,
I HEARD THE RATTLING NOISE,
AND TO MY ASTONISHMENT
I SAW MY AUNT OTILIA'S BONES
LIFT RIGHT OUT OF HER BODY,
FLOAT THROUGH THE AIR,
AND FLY RIGHT THROUGH THE WINDOW,
ALTHOUGH IT WAS CLOSED.

DE PRONTO,
OÍ EL ESTREPITOSO RUIDO,
Y PARA MI ASOMBRO
VI LOS HUESOS DE MI TÍA OTILIA
ELEVARSE DE SU CUERPO,
FLOTAR A TRAVÉS DEL AIRE,
Y VOLAR A TRAVÉS DE LA VENTANA
A PESAR DE QUE ESTABA CERRADA.

AND HER BODY
STAYED ASLEEP IN BED,
ALTHOUGH WITHOUT ITS BONES.
IT WAS ALL SEPARATE,
LIKE A PUZZLE.

WELL,
MY TEETH WERE CHATTERING,
MY HAIR STOOD UP,
AND MY SKIN WAS WHITE.
I LOOKED AT MY FEET AND SAID,
"FEET, GET READY TO MOVE!"

Y SU CUERPO
PERMANECÍA DORMIDO EN LA CAMA,
AUNQUE SIN HUESOS.
ESTABA TODO HECHO PEDAZOS
COMO UN ROMPECABEZAS.

PUES BIEN,
MIS DIENTES CASTAÑETEABAN,
SE ME PUSIERON LOS PELOS DE PUNTA
Y MI PIEL PALIDECIÓ.
ME MIRÉ LOS PIES Y DIJE:
—¡PIES, ÉCHENSE A CORRER!

I JUMPED OUT OF BED SO FAST THAT I KNOCKED THE PIECES
OF AUNT OTILIA'S BODY ONTO THE FLOOR.
SHE WAS STILL MY AUNT, AFTER ALL,
AND ALTHOUGH I WAS SHAKING
I TRIED TO PUT HER PIECES
BACK IN ORDER.

SALTÉ DE LA CAMA TAN RÁPIDO QUE TIRÉ DE UN GOLPE LOS TROZOS
DEL CUERPO DE TÍA OTILIA AL SUELO.
ERA MI TÍA DESPUÉS DE TODO Y,
AUNQUE ESTABA TEMBLANDO,
TRATE DE PONER LOS TROZOS
EN ORDEN.

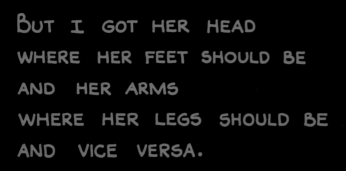

BUT I GOT HER HEAD
WHERE HER FEET SHOULD BE
AND HER ARMS
WHERE HER LEGS SHOULD BE
AND VICE VERSA.

JUST THEN I HEARD HER VOICE.
"OH, YOU BAD BOY.
PUT MY PIECES BACK RIGHT!"
HER BONES WERE FLOATING
OUTSIDE THE WINDOW.
AND I WAS TOO FRIGHTENED
TO MOVE.

PERO PUSE LA CABEZA
DONDE DEBERÍAN ESTAR LOS PIES
Y LOS BRAZOS
DONDE DEBERÍAN ESTAR LAS PIERNAS
Y VICEVERSA.

JUSTAMENTE ENTONCES OÍ SU VOZ:
—¡OH, MUCHACHO TRAVIESO!
¡ACOMODA BIEN MIS PEDAZOS!
LOS HUESOS ESTABAN FLOTANDO
FUERA DE LA VENTANA.
Y YO ESTABA DEMASIADO ASUSTADO
PARA CORRER.

THE SUN WAS COMING UP AND
HER BONES WERE FADING AWAY.
HER VOICE WAS GETTING FARTHER AWAY.
HER PIECES WERE FADING AWAY.
HER SUITCASES WERE FADING AWAY.
AND SHE WAS GONE IN THE MORNING
LIKE A BAD DREAM.

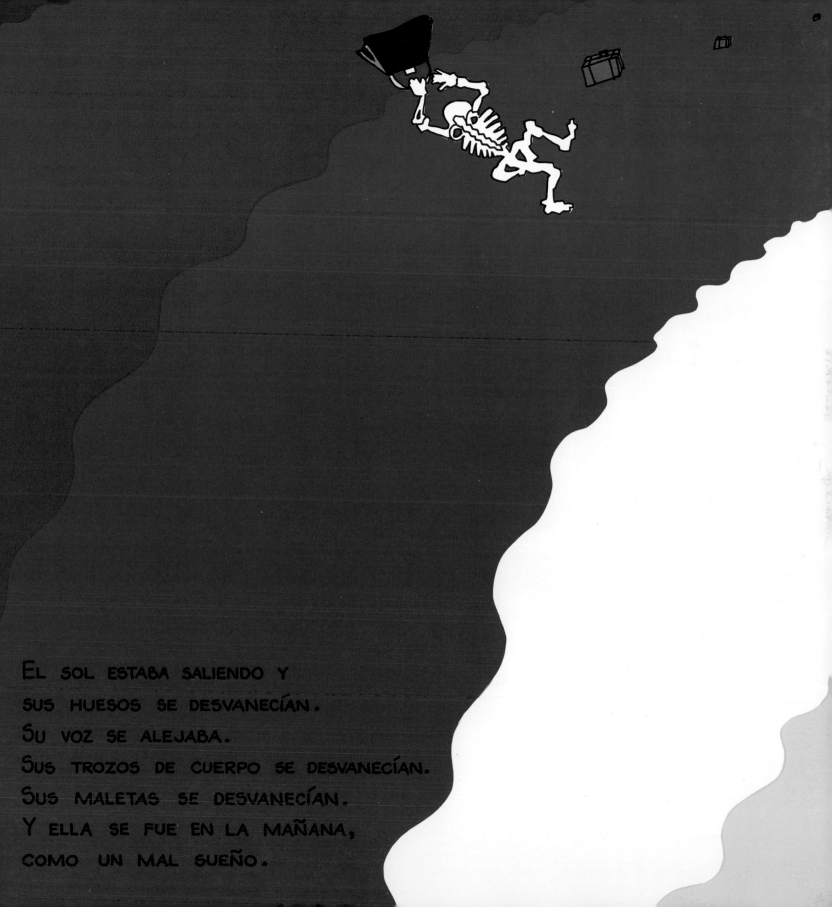

EL SOL ESTABA SALIENDO Y
SUS HUESOS SE DESVANECÍAN.
SU VOZ SE ALEJABA.
SUS TROZOS DE CUERPO SE DESVANECÍAN.
SUS MALETAS SE DESVANECÍAN.
Y ELLA SE FUE EN LA MAÑANA,
COMO UN MAL SUEÑO.

I REALLY CAUGHT A SPANKING
FOR CHASING MY AUNT OTILIA AWAY.
BUT A MONTH LATER WE GOT
A POSTCARD FROM PUERTO RICO.
AUNT OTILIA SAID SHE ENJOYED
HER VISIT AND WAS FINE,
ALTHOUGH SHE FELT A LITTLE MIXED UP.

SHE ALSO SAID SHE WOULDN'T BE ABLE
TO VISIT US AGAIN.
I WAS GLAD.

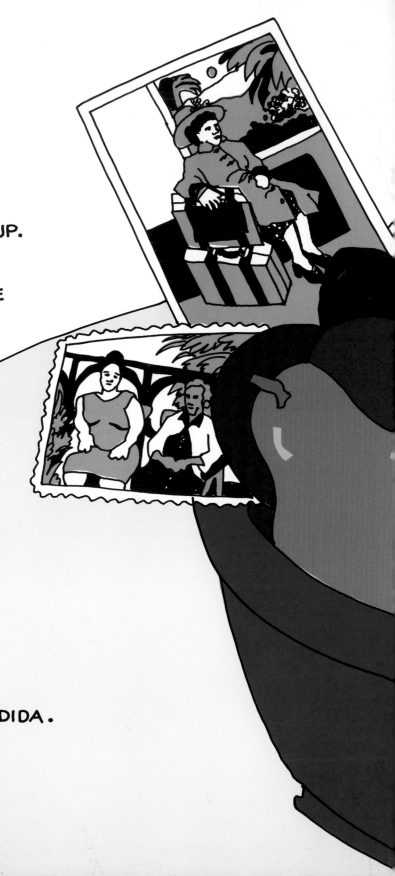

ME DIERON UNAS BUENAS NALGADAS
POR ASUSTAR A MI TÍA OTILIA.
PERO UN MES DESPUÉS RECIBIMOS
UNA TARJETA POSTAL DE PUERTO RICO.
TÍA OTILIA DECÍA QUE HABÍA GOZADO
DE SU VISITA Y QUE ESTABA BIEN,
AUNQUE SE SENTÍA UN POCO CONFUNDIDA.

TAMBIÉN DIJO QUE NO PODRÍA
VISITARNOS DE NUEVO.
¡CÓMO ME ALEGRÉ!

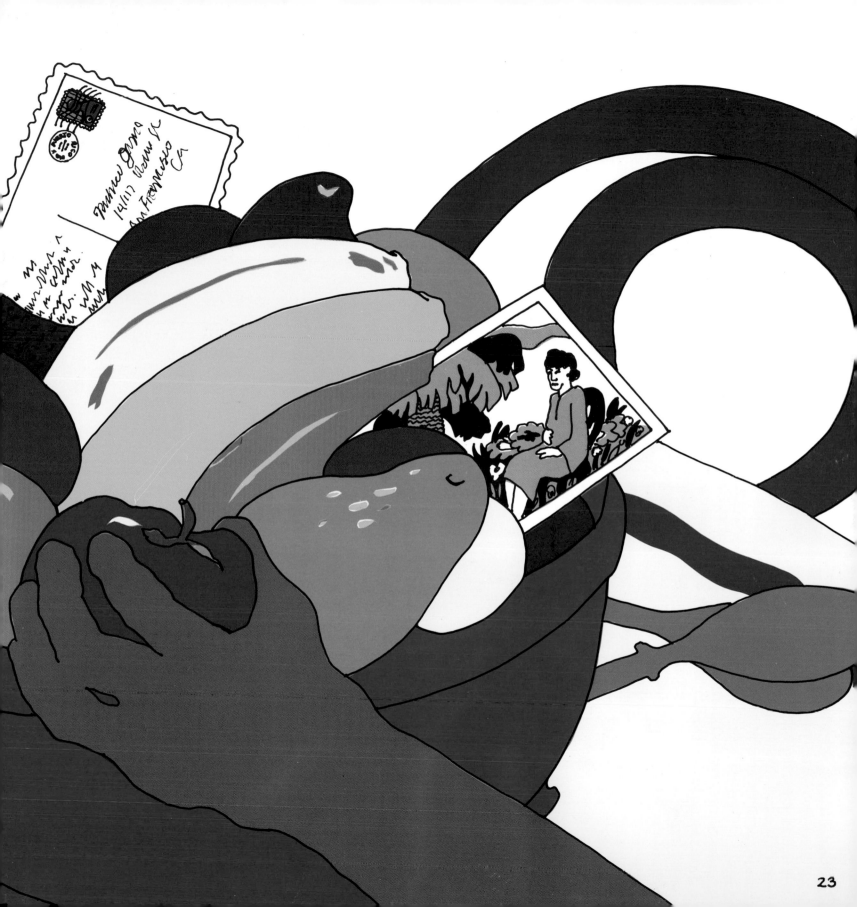

The Author Talks about his Story

I was born in San Francisco of a Mexican mother and a Puerto Rican father. I have been to Mexico a couple of times, but I have yet to visit Puerto Rico.

Like all stories, this one is based on a kernel of fact ~~ and that is that my Aunt Otilia was accompanied by bed shakings and wall knockings wherever she went. However, this was not regarded as unusual in my family, or a cause for much concern. The supernatural had a natural place in our life. Most of the time we ignored it ~~ sometimes it meant something ~~ as in the case of an omen or a dream. We had a large and well-worn copy of an old dream book ~~ and this was often consulted in the morning if a dream seemed signifigant. The approaching death of a family member was often announced by a strong smell of flowers in the house when there were no flowers present. And those who had died were never thought of as being very far away ~~ and were often spoken to as if they were in the room.

My Aunt Otilia did visit us again. In fact, she lives here in San Francisco now. The Puerto Rican and Mexican sides of my family are very different. The Mexicans seem more somber, and the Puerto Ricans tend to be better dancers. I grew up thinking of myself as a Mexican American, and am only recently beginning to think of myself as a Mexi-Rican. This seems like a good combination ~~ and I plan to visit with my cousins in Puerto Rico soon.

Richard García

Series Editor	Harriet Rohmer
Layout/Hand Lettering	Roger I Reyes
Book Design	Harriet Rohmer, Robin Cherin, Roger I Reyes
Production	Robin Cherin
Editorial Assistance	Alma Flor Ada

Library of Congress Cataloging-in-Publication Data
García, Richard, 1941- My Aunt Otilia's spirits = Los espíritus de mi Tía Otilia.
    (Fifth world tales = Cuentos del quinto mundo)
    English and Spanish.
    Summary: When tall, skinny Aunt Otilia comes to visit from Puerto Rico, her curious nephew finds out about her magical powers.
    1. Spanish language — Readers. [1. Psychical research — Fiction. 2. Aunts — Fiction. 3. Puerto Ricans — United States — Fiction. 4. Spanish language materials — Bilingual] I. Cherin, Robin, ill. II. Reyes, Roger I., ill. III. Title. IV. Title: Espíritus de mi Tía Otilia. V. Series: Fifth world tales.
PC4115.G335 1986   468.6'421   86-17129
ISBN 0-89239-029-8